Francis Frith's
AROUND BATH

PHOTOGRAPHIC MEMORIES

Francis Frith's
AROUND BATH

Martin Andrew

FRITH
BOOK Co

British Library Cataloguing in Publication Data

Around Bath
Martin Andrew
ISBN 1-85937-097-7

Frith Book Company Ltd
Frith's Barn, Teffont,
Salisbury, Wiltshire SP3 5QP
Tel: +44 (0) 1722 716 376
Email: www.frithbook.co.uk or info@frithbook.co.uk

Printed and bound in Great Britain

CONTENTS

FRANCIS FRITH: *Victorian Pioneer*

FRANCIS FRITH, Victorian founder of the world-famous photographic archive, was a complex and multitudinous man. A devout Quaker and a highly successful Victorian businessman, he was both philosophic by nature and pioneering in outlook.

By 1855 Francis Frith had already established a wholesale grocery business in Liverpool, and sold it for the astonishing sum of £200,000, which is the equivalent today of over £15,000,000. Now a multi-millionaire, he was able to indulge his passion for travel. As a child he had pored over travel books written by early explorers, and his fancy and imagination had been stirred by family holidays to the sublime mountain regions of Wales and Scotland. 'What a land of spirit-stirring and enriching scenes and places!' he had written. He was to return to these scenes of grandeur in later years to 'recapture the thousands of vivid and tender memories', but with a different purpose. Now in his thirties, and captivated by the new science of photography, Frith set out on a series of pioneering journeys to the Nile regions that occupied him from 1856 until 1860.

INTRIGUE AND ADVENTURE

He took with him on his travels a specially-designed wicker carriage that acted as both dark-room and sleeping chamber. These far-flung journeys were packed with intrigue and adventure. In his life story, written when he was sixty-three, Frith tells of being held captive by bandits, and of fighting 'an awful midnight battle to the very point of surrender with a deadly pack of hungry, wild dogs'. Sporting flowing Arab costume, Frith arrived at Akaba by camel seventy years before Lawrence, where he encountered 'desert princes and rival sheikhs, blazing with jewel-hilted swords'.

During these extraordinary adventures he was assiduously exploring the desert regions bordering the Nile and patiently recording the antiquities and peoples with his camera. He was the first photographer to venture beyond the sixth cataract. Africa was still the mysterious 'Dark Continent', and Stanley and Livingstone's historic meeting was a decade into the future. The conditions for picture taking confound belief. He laboured for hours in his wicker dark-room in the sweltering heat of the desert, while the volatile chemicals fizzed dangerously in their trays. Often he was forced to work in remote tombs and caves where conditions were cooler. Back in London he exhibited his photographs and was 'rapturously cheered' by members of the Royal Society. His reputation as a photographer was made overnight. An eminent modern historian has likened their impact on the population of the time to that on our own generation of the first photographs taken on the surface of the moon.

VENTURE OF A LIFE-TIME

◆ ◆

Characteristically, Frith quickly spotted the opportunity to create a new business as a specialist publisher of photographs. He lived in an era of immense and sometimes violent change. For the poor in the early part of Victoria's reign work was a drudge and the hours long, and people had precious little free time to enjoy themselves.

Most had no transport other than a cart or gig at their disposal, and had not travelled far beyond the boundaries of their own town or village. However, by the 1870s, the railways had threaded their way across the country, and Bank Holidays and half-day Saturdays had been made obligatory by Act of Parliament. All of a sudden the ordinary working man and his family were able to enjoy days out and see a little more of the world.

With characteristic business acumen, Francis Frith foresaw that these new tourists would enjoy having souvenirs to commemorate their days out. In 1860 he married Mary Ann Rosling and set out with the intention of photographing every city, town and village in Britain. For the next thirty years he travelled the country by train and by pony and trap, producing fine photographs of seaside resorts and beauty spots that were keenly bought by millions of Victorians. These prints were painstakingly pasted into family albums and pored over during the dark nights of winter, rekindling precious memories of summer excursions.

THE RISE OF FRITH & CO

◆ ◆

Frith's studio was soon supplying retail shops all over the country. To meet the demand he gathered about him a small team of photographers, and published the work of independent artist-photographers of the calibre of Roger Fenton and Francis Bedford. In order to gain some understanding of the scale of Frith's business one only has to look at the catalogue issued by Frith & Co in 1886: it runs to some 670

pages, listing not only many thousands of views of the British Isles but also many photographs of most European countries, and China, Japan, the USA and Canada – note the sample page shown above from the hand-written *Frith & Co* ledgers detailing pictures taken. By 1890 Frith had created the greatest specialist photographic publishing company in the world, with over 2,000 outlets – more than the combined number that Boots and WH Smith have today! The picture on the right shows the *Frith & Co* display board at Ingleton in the Yorkshire Dales. Beautifully constructed with mahogany frame and gilt inserts, it could display up to a dozen local scenes.

POSTCARD BONANZA

The ever-popular holiday postcard we know today took many years to develop. In 1870 the Post Office issued the first plain cards, with a pre-printed stamp on one face. In 1894 they allowed other publishers' cards to be sent through the mail with an attached adhesive halfpenny stamp. Demand grew rapidly, and in 1895 a new size of postcard was permitted called the court card, but there was little room for illustration. In 1899, a year after Frith's death, a new card measuring 5.5 x 3.5 inches became the standard format, but it was not until 1902 that the divided back came into being, with address and message on one face and a full-size illustration on the other. *Frith & Co* were in the vanguard of postcard development, and Frith's sons Eustace and Cyril continued their father's monumental task, expanding the number of views offered to the public and recording more and more places in Britain, as the coasts and countryside were opened up to mass travel.

Francis Frith died in 1898 at his villa in Cannes, his great project still growing. The archive he created continued in business for another seventy years. By 1970 it contained over a third of a million pictures of 7,000 cities, towns and villages. The massive photographic record Frith has left to us stands as a living monument to a special and very remarkable man.

Frith's Archive: *A Unique Legacy*

FRANCIS FRITH'S legacy to us today is of immense significance and value, for the magnificent archive of evocative photographs he created provides a unique record of change in 7,000 cities, towns and villages throughout Britain over a century and more. Frith and his fellow studio photographers revisited locations many times down the years to update their views, compiling for us an enthralling and colourful pageant of British life and character.

We tend to think of Frith's sepia views of Britain as nostalgic, for most of us use them to conjure up memories of places in our own lives with which we have family associations. It often makes us forget that to Francis Frith they were records of daily life as it was actually being lived in the cities, towns and villages of his day. The Victorian age was one of great and often bewildering change for ordinary people, and though the pictures evoke an impression of slower times, life was as busy and hectic as it is today.

We are fortunate that Frith was a photographer of the people, dedicated to recording the minutiae of everyday life. For it is this sheer wealth of visual data, the painstaking chronicle of changes in dress, transport, street layouts, buildings, housing, engineering and landscape that captivates us so much today. His remarkable images offer us a powerful link with the past and with the lives of our ancestors.

TODAY'S TECHNOLOGY

Computers have now made it possible for Frith's many thousands of images to be accessed almost instantly. In the Frith archive today, each photograph is carefully 'digitised' then stored on a CD Rom. Frith archivists can locate a single photograph amongst thousands within seconds. Views can be catalogued and sorted under a variety of categories of place and content to the immediate benefit of researchers. Inexpensive reference prints can be created for them at the touch of a mouse button, and a wide range of books and other printed materials assembled and published for a wider, more general readership - in the next twelve months over a hundred Frith local history titles will be published! The

See Frith at www. frithbook.co.uk

day-to-day workings of the archive are very different from how they were in Francis Frith's time: imagine the herculean task of sorting through eleven tons of glass negatives as Frith had to do to locate a particular sequence of pictures! Yet the archive still prides itself on maintaining the same high standards of excellence laid down by Francis Frith, including the painstaking cataloguing and indexing of every view.

It is curious to reflect on how the internet now allows researchers in America and elsewhere greater instant access to the archive than Frith himself ever enjoyed. Many thousands of individual views can be called up on screen within seconds on one of the Frith internet sites, enabling people living continents away to revisit the streets of their ancestral home town, or view places in Britain where they have enjoyed holidays. Many overseas researchers welcome the chance to view special theme selections, such as transport, sports, costume and ancient monuments.

We are certain that Francis Frith would have heartily approved of these modern developments, for he himself was always working at the very limits of Victorian photographic technology.

THE VALUE OF THE ARCHIVE TODAY

Because of the benefits brought by the computer, Frith's images are increasingly studied by social historians, by researchers into genealogy and ancestry, by architects, town planners, and by teachers and schoolchildren involved in local history projects. In addition, the archive offers every one of

us a unique opportunity to examine the places where we and our families have lived and worked down the years. Immensely successful in Frith's own era, the archive is now, a century and more on, entering a new phase of popularity.

THE PAST IN TUNE WITH THE FUTURE

Historians consider the Francis Frith Collection to be of prime national importance. It is the only archive of its kind remaining in private ownership and has been valued at a million pounds. However, this figure is now rapidly increasing as digital technology enables more and more people around the world to enjoy its benefits.

Francis Frith's archive is now housed in an historic timber barn in the beautiful village of Teffont in Wiltshire. Its founder would not recognize the archive office as it is today. In place of the many thousands of dusty boxes containing glass plate negatives and an all-pervading odour of photographic chemicals, there are now ranks of computer screens. He would be amazed to watch his images travelling round the world at unimaginable speeds through network and internet lines.

The archive's future is both bright and exciting. Francis Frith, with his unshakeable belief in making photographs available to the greatest number of people, would undoubtedly approve of what is being done today with his lifetime's work. His photographs, depicting our shared past, are now bringing pleasure and enlightenment to millions around the world a century and more after his death.

BATH – *An Introduction*

'Oh, who can ever be tired of Bath?' Jane Austen, 'Northanger Abbey'

BATH IS RIGHTLY designated a UNESCO World Heritage Site. It is perhaps the most remarkably architecturally unified town in England, a quite outstanding example of Georgian town planning, and moreover the vision of a father and son, John Wood the Elder and John Wood the Younger. Their vision was carried on by inspired architects like Thomas Baldwin in the later 18th century, and was even respected by the late-Victorian architect, John Brydon. Who can forget the stunning architectural impact of the vast Royal Crescent or the sinuously curving Lansdown Crescent? From about 1720 to the 1820s, a unique and mercifully complete Georgian city both overlaid the medieval city and expanded to the north, the east and to a lesser extent the south of this town, which is situated on a bend of the River Avon, thirteen miles east of the second city of the country, Bristol.

The Woods' extraordinary and dynamic vision built Bath, but its success as a spa town owed as much to the 'King' of Bath, Richard 'Beau' Nash, who presided over its social suc-

cess for nigh on half a century until his death in 1761. He 'by the force of Genius .. erected the City of BATH into a Province of Pleasure, and became by universal Consent its Legislator, and Ruler'; the city was 'able to vie with any city in Europe, in the politeness of its amusements, and the elegance of its accommodations'. Queen Anne had taken the waters in 1702, and this regal endorsement set the city on its way. However, it is easy walking through the Georgian streets, squares, circuses and crescents to forget that the city had already had a long and illustrious history, and we will look at that before returning to the 18th century.

The city's origins go back well before the Roman conquest of Britain in the 1st century AD. It appears that the springs were sacred to the Celtic Goddess, Sul. It is not surprising; these hot springs on the site of the city issue forth over a quarter of a million gallons each and every day, and they must have appeared a marvel of nature. The ancients clearly took a view that is still held today that if the waters tasted awful (and they do) they must be curative! When the Roman conquerors arrived after the invasion of 43 AD, they rapidly conquered south and east England; they constructed a military road from Lincoln to Axminster, completed by 47 AD, as a temporary frontier, beyond which they soon advanced as far north as Scotland. This road still exists, and is known by its Anglo-Saxon name, the Fosse Way. The Roman military engineers brought it from Cirencester in the Cotswolds to cross the Avon at Bath before heading south-west towards Devon.

Presumably the Romans heard about the mineral waters and the shrine to Sul. Being great assimilators of native deities, they rapidly took over the cult's springs and turned Sul into their own goddess, Minerva. Bath, or rather Aquae Sulis, the 'waters of Sul', very rapidly became noted throughout Britannia and Gaul (modern day France), and thousands of the ill flocked here for cures for rheumatic and similar diseases. The Romans built a very impressive collection of bath houses and pool buildings, over three hundred feet long by one hundred and fifty wide. There was an oval, a circular and a square bath, but the largest, a rectangular one, was only rediscovered in 1880. Lead-lined, it had steps into it from the sides and was surrounded by colonnades. Later it was vaulted over with stone. The bases of the piers remain, and also the bath itself, of course, which is fed by hot springs at a constant 50 degrees Celsius. In 1897 John Brydon constructed an appropriately Roman building around the newly discovered bath, open to the sky.

There was also an important temple dedicated to Sul-Minerva, and fragments of this have come to light; by far the most important of these were the remnants of its main pediment, found in 1790 during building works for Thomas Baldwin's Pump Room. It is of the highest, indeed metropolitan, quality, and depicts the snake-haired and bearded

Gorgon's head on the shield of Minerva, which is supported by two winged Victories - which I suppose must have been confused for angels when it was first found.

After the Roman legions left around 410 AD, the town's fortunes declined and the baths fell into ruin. In 577 AD the Anglo-Saxon Chronicle reports that Bath, along with 973 AD; also, in 1013 Swein Forkbeard, King of Denmark, accepted the fealty of the west of England at Bath. In the 11th century the fortunes of the town revived, and the abbey, now a Benedictine monastery, became one of the most important in England. After the Norman Conquest, it became the seat of a bishopric in 1088 and a large Norman church

the old Roman towns of Gloucester and Cirencester, fell to the Saxons Cuthwine and Ceawlin, after a mighty battle at nearby Dyrham; in the process no less than three British kings were killed. In 603 AD St Augustine passed through, and by 676 AD the monastery established in the city received its first royal endowments of land. The Anglo-Saxon period was one of relative obscurity for the decaying town, although King Edgar was crowned king here at a great assembly in May was built. The present Abbey church was built on the site of the Norman nave only; it is obviously much smaller than its great Norman predecessor, fragments of which remain incorporated in the east end.

Bishop King commissioned the leading court architects of the day, Robert and William Vertue, to design the new church, and it rose slowly from 1499 onwards, a magnificent Perpendicular Gothic building with a fine central tower. The church was a victim of the dissolution of the monasteries in 1539; work stuttered and stopped, and the nave was only roofed (in timber rather than stone) in the early 17th century. The present stone vaults over the nave are 19th century.

The medieval town was a prosperous one, being in the centre of a wool and cloth producing area with a river to carry exports to Bristol. Indeed, it was still important in 1700, when the town began its new life as a centre of fashionable health and leisure pursuits. Unfortunately, very little of the medieval town survives, apart of course from some of its street plan. The Abbey is by far the biggest medieval artefact: otherwise, there is only the much-altered 15th-century church of St Mary Magdalen and a bit of the town wall. There is physically little left from the Tudor and Stuart periods up to the Restoration of Charles II either.

The waters, however, had been taken from the 15th century on; the King's Bath was the focus, mostly of immersion but also of a certain amount of drinking of the waters (not from the bath itself, I should add). The 1597 spring, or well top, of the bath was replicated a century ago as its centrepiece, and there is a famous print of men and women enjoying themselves in the King's Bath together: shocking behaviour to Beau Nash, the Arbiter of Elegance.

However, it is to the 18th century that we must return, for this is very much the focus of this book. The city was in effect rebuilt, replanned and greatly expanded to accommodate the fashionable visitors who soon flocked to the city to take the waters, to gamble, to attend assemblies and generally to enjoy themselves for the Bath 'season'. Huge numbers of houses were built, mainly to rent

to the visitors. Fortunes were made (and lost) by landowners, speculative builders and architects. Indeed, one of the best architects to work in and for the city, Thomas Baldwin, went bankrupt.

Beau Nash organised and presided over the fashionable throng, while John Wood the Elder, scathing of the architecture put up before he settled in the city in 1727, provided the architectural genius to turn a provincial city into a 'New Rome'. This was possibly at the instigation of Ralph Allen, who owned Bath stone quarries and was involved in moves to make the River Avon navigable to Bristol. He encouraged Wood 'to turn his Thoughts towards the Improvement of the City by Building'. In 1725, while still living in Yorkshire, Wood produced his first draft plan to develop land owned in the main by Robert Gay.

Wood started with Queen Square in 1728, where he designed each side as what became known as 'palace fronts'. This was an idea he probably copied from 1720 terraces in London's Grosvenor Square: the terrace houses, usually three windows or bays wide, are built as if a they are a vast palace facade with a centrepiece, usually pedimented, and with the end houses treated as end pavilions. This rapidly became the norm, not only in Bath but elsewhere in England, and helped significantly in giving the townscape great dignity and coherence. He built the 'Grand Place of Assembly to be called the Royal Forum of Bath', now called (rather less grandiosely) North Parade and South Parade, and much else besides. His other great design was the King's Circus, now just called the Circus, which he had just started building when he died in May 1754. His son, also called John and born in Bath in 1727, took over; he completed the Circus, and designed that remarkable and unequalled tour de force, the Royal Crescent of 1767-74, probably the first crescent in England. The Woods also designed public buildings: the younger John was responsible for the New Assembly Rooms and the Hot Bath, for example.

Sadly, Wood the Younger died at the height of his powers and at a relatively young age in 1781. However, other architects and developers took up the palm, including Thomas Baldwin, Richard Eveleigh, John Palmer and, in the 19th century, Henry Goodridge and John Brydon. The Georgian legacy is, however, what makes Bath great. It is very much one of the finest cities in England, if not in Europe. The second and third chapters of this book are designed to be followed as itineraries through the best of the town. The photographs, predominantly pre-World War II, give a picture of the town before bombs and demolitions changed parts of it horribly. However, the areas of destruction were somewhat limited to the south part of the city; the walking routes I have selected predominantly avoid much of this area.

The first route, in Chapter 2, concentrates on the area of the old city, starting near Parade Gardens, progressing via the Baths, Bath Street and an excursion down the rebuilt Southgate to the rebuilt Churchill Bridge. The route goes back into the old city via High Street and Milsom Street, and ends at George Street. The second route, in Chapter 3, is focussed on the post-1720 expansion, and goes through most of the architectural tours de force. It starts where Wood the Elder started, in Queen Square,

then to The Circus and the Royal Crescent and Victoria Park, before starting the more testing part of the itinerary uphill to the later crescents and terraces, including Lansdown and Camden. The views are well worth the climb; then we descend to The Paragon and London Road, before crossing the river into Bathwick and Great Pulteney Street.

Bomb damage and demolition did cause problems, and the architectural response to the challenge was often disastrous. The Hilton Hotel must be the worst possible insult to an historic town, while The Mall shopping centre is hardly less so. Attempts to improve, such as the gimmicky Podium Shopping Centre, only serve to highlight the effortless quality and 'rightness' of the Georgian architects who plied their trade to create this unique city. Manvers Street, New Orchard Street and Southgate suffered particularly, not only from demolitions, both wartime and deliberate, but also from rebuilding in the 1960s and 1970s, two decades of architectural indifference.

The fourth chapter takes us out of the city on a tour of the north, east and south environs, starting at upper Weston, going eastwards to Batheaston, south as far as Limpley Stoke in Wiltshire, and west to Wellow. This gives a good idea of the surroundings of the city, and rounds off the book. I have known and visited Bath for over thirty years, and its architecture and townscape never cease to stun me. I have looked down over the city from Bathampton Down, and have walked the hills and valleys of the Avon and Midford Brook over the years. I hope the views in this book give you as much pleasure as the city has given me.

FROM RAINBOW WOODS 1929 82328

Looking west from Bathampton Down, past the villas of Bathwick across the northern half of the city, we can see how the formality of the ramrod-straight Great Pulteney Street to the left contrasts with, in the right distance below the woods, the sinuous curves of Lansdown Crescent, and other long curving terraces that take advantage of the contours.

GENERAL VIEW C1886 6997

Taken from near the Wells Road above the south bank of the River Avon, this is an archive view, for much was destroyed in the Baedeker and other bombing raids during World War II. The Abbey on the left and the spire of St John the Baptist Church act as reference points; the latter was severely bomb-damaged in 1942.

VIEW FROM THE ABBEY 1929 82323

Closer in to the centre of the city, this view from the roof of the Abbey looks north along the High Street with the domed Georgian Guildhall on the right. The other dome to its right belongs to the covered market. Beyond is the quirky 1830s St Nicholas' parish church, now with the very modern Podium Shopping centre to its right.

GENERAL VIEW c1965 B33027

This view, from near the greatly-expanded village of Weston, now thoroughly engrossed into Bath, looks eastward to the tree-fringed ridge of Bathampton Down. Bathampton village is on its left slopes, while the city is to the right, largely hidden in the winding Avon valley.

THE ROMAN BATHS 1890 25135

The Roman town of Aquae Sulis had as its focus the hot spring-fed baths, where citizens of the Empire flocked for rheumatic cures. The baths the Romans built were indeed sumptuous, and the remains give one some idea of their scale and quality. This fascinating early view shows the Roman Baths before Brydon's 1897 alterations and new buildings.

THE ROMAN BATHS 1897 40789
In 1897 the architect John Brydon added these dignified colonnades around the baths with their balustrades and statues. Wisely, he avoided placing his slender Doric columns on the much larger Roman bases and stumps of piers that line the edges of the bath and are linked by steps leading into the water.

THE ROMAN BATHS 1901 46468
The quality of Brydon's work is well brought out in this view; I have heard visitors commenting on the remarkable survival of so much Roman work! Note the fountain in the centre of the bath, and the pile of Roman masonry in the shadows beyond.

THE ROMAN BATHS, SCULPTURE FROM TEMPLE OF MINERVA 1907 57725

The Romans quickly absorbed the local Celtic goddess, 'Sul', into the cult of Minerva, and built a temple here in Sul-Minerva's honour as patroness of the baths. This astounding sculpture was dug up in 1790 below the Pump Room, and shows a snake-haired Gorgon on Minerva's shield. It obviously came from the temple pediment, and is now in the British Museum.

THE ROMAN BATHS 1907 57723

Although most associate Bath's waters with the Georgian or Roman period, the spring-fed baths were very popular in Tudor and Stuart times. The King's Bath, seen here, dates from 1597, but little survives of the original. The ornate stone wellhead in the centre of the bath copies that in a well-known 17th-century print showing scenes of uninhibited mixed bathing.

THE ABBEY
West Front

Remarkably little of the medieval city survives; apart from St Mary Magdalen and a fragment of town wall, the Abbey is the main physical evidence of what was a prosperous town built on the wool trade. However, the superb, and very late medieval, Abbey church more than compensates. Note the genuine 'Bath chair' in this view.

THE ABBEY c1965

Although fragments of the Norman abbey remain, the present abbey church dates from 1499, and was a prodigiously long time a-building: the nave was still roofless into the 17th century. A great Perpendicular Gothic church, its west front is famous for the ladders with angels ascending and descending each side of the towering west window.

THE ABBEY, WEST FRONT 1887   19583

THE ABBEY c1965   B33007

THE ABBEY 1911 63682
The abbey is much shorter than its Norman
predecessor, occupying only the space of its nave; the
former choir and transepts were where the railinged
green is in this view. The tower, 162 feet high, and the
rich roofscape of crocketted pinnacles and pierced
battlements, dominate the town.

THE ABBEY 1925 76763

This area is now somewhat traffic-plagued, so that this peaceful scene is no more; the obelisk to the Prince of Orange, erected by Beau Nash in 1734 (restored in 1872), now occupies a railing-less traffic island. Behind the obelisk and the trees is Orange Grove, early 18th-century, but titivated in 1897 with eleven gables and shell-hoods to all the first floor windows.

THEATRE ROYAL c1965 B33009

The entrance block of the theatre was formed from Beau Nash's first house in Bath, a pre-Wood era building of 1720 with heavy moulded window surrounds and cornices. Beyond the bust of Garrick, out of view, is the unoriginally-named Garrick's Head pub. The swagger front of the theatre actually faces Beauford Square, and was started in 1805.

ST MICHAEL'S CHURCH 1895 35753
Replacing a medieval church that lay beyond the walled town's north gate, now commemorated by the street's name of Northgate Street, this church by Manners was started in 1835 in an early inaccurate Gothic Revival style: playfully un-medieval, but clearly cocking a snook at the Georgian architecture all around it, it was the first of several Victorian Gothic churches built in the city.

THE WATER FOUNTAIN 1909 61531

The colonnaded street behind, part of the 1789 Bath Improvement Act scheme, is an elegant piece of Georgian town planning. It is very close to architectural perfection: the effect is marred by notices and posters (note that for artificial teeth in a first floor window,) and comprehensively so by the fountain in the foreground. This was installed in 1839, but is now removed to Terrace Walk.

THE MUNICIPAL BUILDINGS AND THE ABBEY 1896 38360

The Georgian Guildhall to the right, designed by Thomas Baldwin in 1777, was greatly enlarged to the designs of John Brydon in 1893. In this view the northern wing, which turns the corner into Bridge Street, is still virtually brand new. Brydon certainly caught the spirit of Baldwin's Adam-esque masterpiece, only departing from it in the Baroque towers at each end.

THE MUNICIPAL BUILDINGS 1895 38361

Here Brydon's wings, still fresh, flank the 1777 centre with its figure of Justice, for once not blindfolded, crowning the pediment. The dome behind was another felicitous touch by Brydon. One would hardly know the wings were not Georgian originals: praise indeed. The Baroque-influenced towers add rich emphases to the frontage.

THE GRAND PUMP ROOM HOTEL 1901 46476

In 1869 the Grand Pump Room Hotel opened. Designed by Wilson and Wilcox, its ponderous late Georgian style had the side wings topped by Frenchified pavilion roofs. It closed the vista west along Abbey Churchyard from the Abbey's west front, past the Pump Room, and through the north Colonnade. Demolished in 1959, it was replaced by pallid Neo-Georgian work.

PULTENEY BRIDGE C1965 B33155

Designed by Robert Adam and built between 1769 and 1774, this Palladian bridge was built for Sir William Pulteney to link his Bathwick estate to the city. Adam adapted Palladio's own design for a bridge with shops and houses to produce an elegant masterpiece. However, it ruined the builder, and parts had to be reconstructed as early as 1804.

VIEW FROM PULTENEY BRIDGE 1914 67450

Looking south from the bridge, the towering mass of the former Empire Hotel is on the right with its terrace. Beyond is the spire of St John the Baptist Church and the Parade Gardens. The bridge is the North Parade Bridge, built in 1836 as a cast-iron structure, as seen here, but since 1936 clad in stone.

FROM THE EMPIRE HOTEL 1935
This view, taken from an upper floor window of the execrable Empire Hotel, looks beyond the Parade Gardens, laid out in the 1880s, to North Parade, a long 'palace front' of twenty-five bays with a central pediment. This was part of John Wood the Elder's Royal Forum of the 1740s, now unfortunately dominated by the interloping Gothic spire of St John the Baptist.

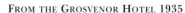

FROM THE GROSVENOR HOTEL 1935
Looking back to the former Empire Hotel, opened in 1901 and a poor counterweight to the Abbey, we see the houses of Terrace Walk on the left, now with ground-floor shops, which faced the Greek temple-style Royal Literary and Scientific Institution of 1806-20. This was swept away in 1933 for the road improvements seen here, still pompous and vandal fresh.

FROM THE EMPIRE HOTEL 1935 86796

FROM THE GROSVENOR HOTEL 1935 86802

NORTH PARADE AND THE ABBEY 1949 B33104
This view, closer in from the junction of North Parade and Pierrepont Street, shows the site of the Royal Literary and Scientific Institution, now a bustling bus station. The balustraded enclosure on the traffic island surrounds steps leading down to The Island Club and the Parade Gardens, formerly known as St James' Triangle.

THE FERNLEY HOTEL 1935 86800A
Now renamed The Abbey Hotel, this terrace of houses became an hotel in 1879. It is part of the elder Wood's Royal Forum, with its long, formal composition fronting North Parade. In the foreground is the then newly-laid-out area replacing the Royal Literary and Scientific Institution, now all paved and occupied by the water fountain of 1839 relocated from Bath Street.

YORK STREET AND THE ROMAN BATHS c1955 B33099

From Terrace Walk, York Street passes the rear of the Roman Baths, screened by the rusticated walls and corner pavilion added by Brydon in the 1890s. The balustrade to the right belongs to buildings demolished to form a square south of the abbey, Abbey Churchyard. The pavilion roof at the top right belongs to the now-demolished Grand Pump Room Hotel.

BATH STREET 1935 86806

This elegant colonnaded street, with its upper storeys supported on slender Ionic columns, is now cleaned and restored, and the distracting fountain has been moved. Bath Street connected the Pump Room with the Cross Bath of 1784, and was designed by Thomas Baldwin; the foundation stone was laid in 1791 as part of the 1789 Bath Improvement Act works.

SOUTHGATE STREET 1904 52994
A few buildings on the left survive, but the rest have gone, apart from the
Abbey pinnacles in the distance. Bombs and demolition saw them off: the
left side was rebuilt in the 1960s, and the right side was replaced by the
dire Mall shopping centre in 1971. The tower was the Georgian St James
church of 1768, whose blitzed ruins were finally demolished in 1957.

THE OLD BRIDGE 1887 19590
Beyond Southgate, on Broad Quays, the 1966 Churchill Bridge over the River Avon replaced the Old Bridge we see in this view. The stonework arches belong to the 1754 replacement for St Lawrence's Bridge; it dated from 1362, and even had a chapel to St Lawrence halfway across. The medieval piers survived, while the ironwork superstructure was Victorian.

THE OLD BRIDGE c1965 B33131
Here we see the Old Bridge just before its replacement by the present bridge; its ironwork superstructure cantilevered the footways out over the river. Behind is the splendid medieval-style railway line of the 1840s raised above the flood plain of the Avon with castellated turrets and battlemented parapets.

ST MICHAEL'S CHURCH 1904 53000
The church is now flanked by different buildings: Rubie's on the left made way in 1928 for the rather good stone-clad neo-Georgian Post Office with its circular porch. Not so lucky to the right: these Georgian buildings were replaced by the Podium Shopping Centre, a gimmicky 1990s semi-literate 'interpretation' of Georgian architecture - but at least it screens the truly awful Hilton Hotel beyond.

CHEAP STREET FROM ORANGE GROVE 1895 35752
Back into town, this view from Orange Grove looks along past Brydon's Municipal Buildings of 1893, 'rendered necessary by the large increase of public business since the erection of the central building the Guildhall 1777' according to the plaque. The shaped gables to the building on the corner of Cheap Street have been replaced by a more correct 'Georgian' parapet.

HIGH STREET AND MUNICIPAL BUILDINGS 1904 52993
This view, taken from the Abbey's aisle roof, again
shows the Guildhall to the right; much of the left
hand side has now been rebuilt, including the
Christopher Hotel, in 1960s bland and cheap neo-
Georgian. At least the replacement buildings are faced
in stone and have sash windows.

UNION STREET 1914 67454
From the High Street, walk down Upper Borough
Walls on the site of the town's medieval north wall to
turn left into Union Street. This view is from the
southern end, looking north along a street designed
and laid out by Thomas Baldwin soon after 1800.
It became a shopping street later in the century, when
many ornate shop fronts were installed.

UNION STREET c1955 B33121

UNION STREET c1955
Union Street is now pedestrianised; this view shows some of the modern shop fronts installed by 1955 which replaced the much better Victorian ones. Fox-Andrews' shop, The Central Supply, established as long ago as 1868, is in both views, but has since been replaced by a shoe shop.

◆

MILSOM STREET 1895
Looking north from New Bond Street, this late 19th-century view captures well the quality of Milsom Street, one of the earlier streets laid out beyond the boundaries of the original walled town. As with most of the city's central streets, Milsom Street was laid out as a residential one, only acquiring shops from about 1800 onwards.

MILSOM STREET 1895 36457

MILSOM STREET 1904 52992
The street was named after Daniel Milsom, a wine cooper who owned the land. It was laid out mainly in the 1760s. The grandest building was Somersetshire Buildings on the right, a terrace of five houses which has pedimented end houses and a central house with a bowed front, all enriched with columns, capitals and cornices.

MILSOM STREET 1925 76754
Built in 1782 to designs by Thomas Baldwin, Somersetshire Buildings remain the most elegant and ornate in the street; the bowed centre house is a total contrast to the regular flat fronts of the other Georgian houses. The building on the right of about 1790 with its columns and pilasters over a rusticated ground storey is now Lloyds Bank-TSB.

MILSOM STREET c1965 B33038

This view looks south down Milsom Street to Old Bond Street. Some of the right hand side is taken up by Jolly's, the famous Bath department store which had a most elaborate Victorian stone and granite shopfront of 1875 added to part of its frontage. Somersetshire Buildings can be seen on the left beyond more standard three-bay Palladian houses.

WOOD STREET c1955 B33118

As we look east from Queen Square, the terrace we see on the right, Northumberland Buildings, built in 1778, is another design by the ubiquitous Thomas Baldwin. The houses on the left retain their elegant columned early 19th-century shopfronts, while the quirky 1850s building beyond is still the premises of Paxton and Whitfield, cheesemongers in Bath since 1797.

YORK HOUSE HOTEL 1907 57720

Moving north to the end of Milsom Street, we see George Street, another good street laid out around 1761. Designed by the younger Wood in the 1760s, York House Hotel has descended to a Slug and Lettuce theme pub and Travelodge. It is now called York Buildings, and a recent stone Doric portico replaces the ornate glazed entrance canopy.

EDGAR BUILDINGS 1935 86804

The north side of George Street is raised above the roadway; at the left is part of Edgar Buildings, completed in 1762, whose centrally-pedimented houses close the vista up Milsom Street. The right-hand building, an Italianate palazzo at the corner of Milsom Street, built in 1865 as a bank, is now the Bath Environmental Centre.

QUEEN SQUARE 1901 46474
Having completed our tour of the central part of the
city, this chapter provides an itinerary taking in the
best of the great terraces, squares and crescents that
were developed to its north. This is Georgian urban
architecture and townscape at its best, and our route
starts in Queen Square, west of Milsom Street.

QUEEN SQUARE c1955 B33117

Queen Square was laid out by John Wood the Elder, and building started in 1728 to his designs. His novel idea was to treat each side of the Square as a single architectural composition, so that the terraces of houses looked like single grand palace fronts with central pediments on three sides of the Square.

THE CIRCUS 1896 38367

A walk up Gay Street, named after Robert Gay, who granted John Wood the lease on this hilly area north-west of the old city, leads to one of the most celebrated pieces of this remarkable city's townscape: The Circus. It is a complete circle, and was laid out by John Wood the Elder in 1754.

THE CIRCUS 1911 63686

It was originally named King's Circus; work started in February 1754, but Wood himself died in May and the work had to be completed by his son, John Wood the Younger. There are three equal and similar blocks, with paired columns flanking each window on each of the three storeys: a Roman circus turned inside out.

THE CIRCUS c1965 B33176

By the mid nineteen-sixties the grime of a coal fire age is beginning to be cleaned off. The central railings went during world War II, and now the tatty chain link fence that replaced it has also gone. The five great plane trees in the centre of the square remain as a focus for this wonderful architectural composition.

THE ROYAL CRESCENT c1965 B33174

Walk along Brock Street, and you reach the quite extraordinary Royal Crescent of John Wood the Younger. Built between 1767 and 1774, it is a breathtakingly monumental semi-ellipse of thirty houses, with one hundred and fourteen giant columns to the two upper floors in its prodigious length of five hundred and thirty eight feet.

VICTORIA PARK BANDSTAND 1925 76761

The Royal Crescent looks out over a field which drops away to Victoria Park beyond, also fields when the Crescent
was built. The Park was laid out by Edward Davis, a pupil of Sir John Soane, the architect of the old Bank of
England, and opened in 1830. This view shows the later bandstand in full swing.

VICTORIA PARK 1920 73971
On each side of the bandstand are stone canopies protecting
marble vases. The inscription tells us they were the gift of the
Emperor Napoleon Bonaparte in 1805 to his Empress,
Josephine. Brought back as spoils of war, they were later
given to the park in 1874, and the columned baldocchinos
were erected by a Captain Huth in 1914.

ROYAL VICTORIA PARK 1911 63691

ROYAL VICTORIA PARK 1911
In the section of the park beyond Marlborough Road, Edward Davis erected this obelisk to the then Princess Victoria in early 1837 for Bath to commemorate the 'attainment of her majority'. The cannon has now gone, but Davis' four pedestrian entrance gateways, two surmounted by Egyptian lions, remain: elegant and Soane-like architecture in a pared-down Greek style.

◆

ST JAMES SQUARE 1929
Back uphill, past Marlborough Buildings, we reach St James Square, altogether more conventional. On a sloping site the houses step up, so the scope for grand palace fronts is limited; the central houses on each side are defined by a modest pediment. Designed by John Palmer and finished by 1794, the three-bay houses are remarkably little changed.

ST JAMES SQUARE 1929 82335

CAVENDISH CRESCENT 1907 57717
From St James Square, continue uphill beside High Common to Cavendish Crescent, which is high enough to have
fine views to the south. Designed by John Pinch for a speculator who went bankrupt, the quadrant was built
between 1815 and 1830. Its perfection is only marred by the Waterloo balcony added to No 9.

LANSDOWN CRESCENT 1896 38366

Along the ridge, Somerset Place and Lansdown Crescent curve sinuously to great architectural effect, with grand views across the city. Lansdown Crescent is one of John Palmer's finest compositions, and dates from 1789 to 1793. It has twenty houses to its centre range with its pedimented central and bow-fronted end houses, flanked by two further ranges of houses.

CAMDEN CRESCENT 1907 57716

From Lansdown Road turn left into Camden Crescent, an ambitious project begun in 1788 on the slopes of Beacon Hill, which gave splendid views eastwards. John Eveleigh, the architect, used columns for the pedimented centrepiece and end 'pavilions', with flat pilasters to the houses in between. Unstable ground meant only four houses were built to the right of the pedimented centre instead of ten.

The Paragon 1911 63684
Continue down Lansdown Road to The Paragon, a superb terrace of twenty-one houses set between two roads on steeply differing levels, their stables and vaults fronting Walcot Street far below. The Paragon's elegant facades face Vineyards, terraces on a raised pavement, with the Countess of Huntingdon Connexion Chapel of 1765, now the Buildings of Bath Museum, in the gap.

THE PARAGON AND GUINEA LANE 1904 52999
Continuing uphill past the end of The Paragon and at the junction with Guinea Lane, Roman Road heads for the junction with a steeply climbing Walcot Street and London Road. In this view, a tram passes the park with an advertisement for Fox-Andrews' shop in Union Street. Many Frith views of Bath around 1904 proudly include the then new electric trams.

WALCOT PARADE c1965 B33231

Reaching London Road, we have P.R. Hayes department store on the right, now expanded from the one shop in this view, and on the left the picturesque Walcot Parade of about 1770, with its vaults for coal cellars and stores beneath the curving raised pavement in front. Unlike many of Bath's terraces, the designs of individual houses are not uniform.

CLEVELAND PLACE AND BRIDGE 1929 82341

Beyond Walcot Parade is Cleveland Place, which forms a forecourt to Cleveland Bridge across the Avon. Splendidly guarded by four toll houses or lodges in Greek temple style with Doric columned porticos, the cast-iron bridge was designed by Henry Goodrich and opened in 1827. On the left is The Dispensary of 1845 with its pediment.

LONDON ROAD 1907 57727
Continue east along London Road to Beaufort Buildings West and East,
long gently curving terraces of 1791 to 1815. The building on the left is
now the First Inn Last Out pub, and the higher building beyond is the
start of Beaufort Buildings. The raised pavement survives, but with
conventional steps instead of the projecting stones of 1907.

GREAT PULTENEY STREET 1887 19589

Go back into town and cross the Pulteney Bridge with its small shops into Argyle Street. At its junction with Laura Place you can look along Great Pulteney Street towards the Holburne Museum, built as the Sydney House hotel in 1796 to serve the Sydney Gardens beyond, a large hexagonal public park now bisected by the railway.

GREAT PULTENEY STREET 1901 46470

In this view the trees are more mature and obscure the long facades of this eleven hundred foot long road. This was part of Thomas Baldwin's ambitious new town between the river and Bathwick of the 1790s, much of which was never built. The fountain of 1880 commemorating the centenary of the Bath and West Show remains, but only just.

PULTENEY HOTEL 1914 67452

The houses on the north corner of Laura Place became an hotel in 1866 and acquired the ornate iron and glass porch early this century. Recently closed as an hotel, it is now apartments named Connaught Mansions; the porch has gone, presumably in the interests of Georgian correctness.

WELLS WAY C1965 B33014

This view of the then new dual carriageway section of the A367 Radstock road, Wells Way, as it drops down from Odd Down towards the city, seems a curious subject for a photograph, but in those far-off days new roads were still exciting. In the distance behind the school are the trees at the top of Beechen Cliff.

NEWBRIDGE ROAD 1909 61539
There was considerable expansion of Bath in the later
19th century along the valley towards Bristol. This view
looks west along Newbridge Road with its terraces of neat
villas. These all survive, albeit now with concrete roof tiles.
Most of the front garden stone walls remain, but the trams
and the overhead cable standards have long gone.

ON THE CANAL 1895 35759

The Kennet and Avon Canal, authorised by Act of Parliament in 1794 and opened in 1810, linked Bristol with London, cutting a canal from the Avon in Bath to the Kennet, which was then canalised to the Thames. This view from the canal towpath looks north to the George Street bridge in Bathwick, with the backs of Sydney Buildings on the right.

VIEW FROM WARMINSTER ROAD BRIDGE 1914 67455

Further along the towpath, past the section through Sydney Gardens, the canal passes under the Warminster Road, almost converging with the Great Western Railway line. In the foreground is the Humane Society's Station. The chur-h tower is that of St Saviour's at Larkhall, consecrated in 1832, with its tall west tower imitating medieval Somerset ones.

UPPER WESTON
High Street 1907

Upper Weston has all the appearance of a typical Cotswold stone village with its main street winding gently uphill. The early 19th-century houses on the left are, however, quite urban in feel and reflect the proximity of Bath. Indeed, Weston is connected to the city via the suburbs of Newbridge, Weston Park and Lower Weston.

CHARLCOMBE
The Church 1907

A total contrast is Charlcombe, a tiny hamlet on a minor road a mere half mile north of the Bath suburb of Fairfield Park. With the grassy downs behind, this is a most delightful medieval church: small and intimate, set in a well treed churchyard, with a most unusual stone bell turret, battlemented and carried on big corbels.

UPPER WESTON, HIGH STREET 1907 57745

CHARLCOMBE, THE CHURCH 1907 57754

BATHEASTON, HIGH STREET c1960 B308019
Heading north-east out of Bath on the A4, cross the A46 junction onto the old A4, which soon becomes Batheaston High Street. This follows the course of a much older road, the Roman 'Fosse Way', which runs from the 'colonia' of Lincoln to Axminster in Devon, built as a military road around 47 AD.

BATHEASTON, STAMBRIDGE c1960 B308025

Further downhill, at Fiveways, the road on the right is Fosse Lane. Here the Roman Fosse Way climbs out of the Avon valley to cross Banner Down on its way to Cirencester, the Roman town of Corinium. Beyond the low stone wall along the left side of the road the land drops to the bank of the River Avon.

BATHEASTON, THE WEIR c1960 B308013

The mill is actually on the Bathampton or south bank of the Avon, beyond the toll bridge. In this view it has been converted into the Weir Tea Garden Hotel, and the meadow turned into a tea lawn. The hotel has since been renamed Bathampton Mill, which is even more confusing, but it is a delightful spot.

BATHAMPTON, THE WEIR 1907 57751

This view looks from the north bank of the Avon, near the toll bridge. The mill buildings are still in use (compare this view with the last one). The toll bridge (cars currently 30p) is just out of picture to the left; indeed, the weir goes beneath its northern arches. Built in 1872, the bridge replaced an old ferry.

BATHFORD, ASHLEY ROAD c1955 B309011

BATHFORD
Ashley Road c1955

Do not cross the toll bridge yet, but retrace your steps through Batheaston to Bathford, for there are few river crossings. This is still a distinct village, with lanes winding uphill, although the wall on the right has now been replaced by a 1970s close, Titan Barrow, the name perpetuating a house of 1748 by Wood the Elder.

—◆—

BATHFORD
Brown's Folly c1955

Dominating the countryside around, and particularly impressive from the Bathampton side of the valley, Brown's Folly was built on the summit ridge of Bathford Hill in 1840. The builder, Wade Brown, was a local quarry owner; woods have now overgrown the local pits and quarries cut into the sides of Bathford Hill.

BATHFORD BROWN'S FOLLY c1955 B309002

BATHAMPTON, THE CHURCH 1907 57748
Across the toll bridge from Batheaston, the road crosses the A4 dual
carriageway Batheaston bypass into Bathampton, a village now linked by
development to Bathwick and Bath. The area round the medieval church is
unspoilt; besides the church, which has a very recent eastern extension, there
is a Victorian school and a fine 18th-century Manor House near the river.

BATHAMPTON, THE CANAL AND THE GEORGE INN 1907 57749
In the 1790s the Kennet and Avon Canal swept past at first floor window level of the 17th-century George Inn to cut it off from the High Street. It also separated the church and Manor House from the village; all were to the right of the canal bridge on which the photographer stood. The factory burned down in 1963.

MONKTON COMBE, THE POST OFFICE c1955 M126010
Back across the river, via the Batheaston toll bridge, follow the Avon south before turning right to Monkton Combe, a delightful village nestling in the valley of the Midford Brook. Much of the south side of the main street beyond the village shop and the junction with Mill Lane is now occupied by a private school, Monkton Combe School.

MONKTON COMBE, THE MILL c1955 M126019
At the end of Mill Lane, across the course of the old Somerset Coal Canal (1794-1898) and past a small 17th-century stone lock-up, is the former water mill. The building on the left, the Old Mill, is a house with an added balcony, while that to the right is now the well known Morris Minor Centre.

MONKTON COMBE, THE VIADUCT c1955 M126021
Go back to the Avon valley, turn right at the traffic lights by the Viaduct Inn, then left towards Lower Limpley Stoke. This view, actually on the main A36, looks across the viaduct over the Midford Brook back to the Viaduct Inn. Three hundred yards further north is Rennie's 1805 Dundas Aqueduct carrying the canal across the River Avon.

LIMPLEY STOKE, THE VILLAGE c1955 L47003

LIMPLEY STOKE
The Village c1955
This Wiltshire village grew up on three roughly parallel terraces on the steep and well-wooded Avon valley side, with the parish church at the south end. This view looks north down the lane to Lower Limpley Stoke, with the railway curving along to the station beyond the locomotive water tower (now closed).

◆

LIMPLEY STOKE
Lower Village c1955
Further down this lane, the centre of Lower Limpley Stoke is reached, with the Hop Pole Inn on the left, the post office and village shop on the right, and the garage beyond, although the Esso sign has now gone. The more urban style of the three-storey shop contrasts with the cottagey Berkeley Cottage in the foreground.

LIMPLEY STOKE, LOWER VILLAGE c1955 L47019

LIMPLEY STOKE, MIDDLE VILLAGE c1955 L47020

On the next 'terrace' up is Middle Limpley Stoke, its narrow winding lane flanked by dry stone and mortared walls. The right hand cottages are dated 1885, and the village hall beyond was built in 1845.

WELLOW, THE MANOR HOUSE AND HIGH STREET c1955 W180004

Climbing out of Limpley Stoke, head west through Hinton Charterhouse with its fascinating remains of the 13th-century Carthusian priory, Hinton Priory, to the village of Wellow, four miles south of Bath. This view looks west along the High Street past the Manor House on the right, a good 17th-century house with a tall gabled three-storey chamber wing.

WELLOW, THE VILLAGE c1955 W180003
This view looks in the opposite direction, east past the Manor House on the left with cottages and the former Ebenezer United Methodist Chapel of 1869 beside the raised and railinged pavement. On the right is St Julian's Primary School, built in 1852 as the Wellow National School in the then usual Gothic style.

WELLOW, HIGH STREET c1955 W180013
Towards the edge of the village are former Rural District Council houses, now with lusher gardens, and opposite is a former Nonconformist chapel dated 1898. The tour of some villages around Bath is now finished, and you can head back northwards to the city.

Index

Frith Book Co Titles

Frith Book Company publish over a 100 new titles each year. For latest catalogue please contact Frith Book Co.

Town Books 96pp, 100 photos. County and Themed Books 128pp, 150 photos
(unless specified) All titles hardback laminated case and jacket
except those indicated pb (paperback)

Around Barnstaple	1-85937-084-5	£12.99
Around Blackpool	1-85937-049-7	£12.99
Around Bognor Regis	1-85937-055-1	£12.99
Around Bristol	1-85937-050-0	£12.99
Around Cambridge	1-85937-092-6	£12.99
Cheshire	1-85937-045-4	£14.99
Around Chester	1-85937-090-X	£12.99
Around Chesterfield	1-85937-071-3	£12.99

Around Maidstone	1-85937-056-X	£12.99
North Yorkshire	1-85937-048-9	£14.99
Around Nottingham	1-85937-060-8	£12.99
Around Penzance	1-85937-069-1	£12.99
Around Reading	1-85937-087-X	£12.99
Around St Ives	1-85937-068-3	£12.99
Around Salisbury	1-85937-091-8	£12.99
Around Scarborough	1-85937-104-3	£12.99
Scottish Castles	1-85937-077-2	£14.99
Around Sevenoaks and Tonbridge	1-85937-057-8	£12.99
Sheffield and S Yorkshire	1-85937-070-5	£14.99
Shropshire	1-85937-083-7	£14.99
Staffordshire	1-85937-047-0 (96pp)	£12.99
Suffolk	1-85937-074-8	£14.99
Surrey	1-85937-081-0	£14.99
Torbay	1-85937-063-2	£12.99
Wiltshire	1-85937-053-5	£14.99

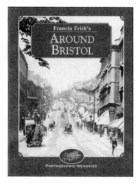
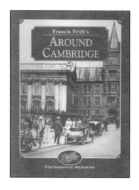

Around Chichester	1-85937-089-6	£12.99
Cornwall	1-85937-054-3	£14.99
Cotswolds	1-85937-099-3	£14.99
Around Derby	1-85937-046-2	£12.99
Devon	1-85937-052-7	£14.99
Dorset	1-85937-075-6	£14.99
Dorset Coast	1-85937-062-4	£14.99
Around Dublin	1-85937-058-6	£12.99
East Anglia	1-85937-059-4	£14.99
Around Eastbourne	1-85937-061-6	£12.99
English Castles	1-85937-078-0	£14.99
Around Falmouth	1-85937-066-7	£12.99
Hampshire	1-85937-064-0	£14.99
Isle of Man	1-85937-065-9	£14.99

British Life A Century Ago
246 x 189mm 144pp, hardback. Black and white Lavishly illustrated with photos from the turn of the century, and with extensive commentary. It offers a unique insight into the social history and heritage of bygone Britain.

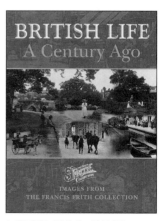

1-85937-103-5 £17.99

Available from your local bookshop or from the publisher

Frith Book Co Titles Available in 2000

Around Bakewell	1-85937-1132	£12.99	Feb
Around Bath	1-85937-097-7	£12.99	Feb
Around Belfast	1-85937-094-2	£12.99	Feb
Around Bournemouth	1-85937-067-5	£12.99	Feb
Cambridgeshire	1-85937-086-1	£14.99	Feb
Essex	1-85937-082-9	£14.99	Feb
Greater Manchester	1-85937-108-6	£14.99	Feb
Around Guildford	1-85937-117-5	£12.99	Feb
Around Harrogate	1-85937-112-4	£12.99	Feb
Hertfordshire	1-85937-079-9	£14.99	Feb
Isle of Wight	1-85937-114-0	£14.99	Feb
Around Lincoln	1-85937-111-6	£12.99	Feb
Margate/Ramsgate	1-85937-116-7	£12.99	Feb
Northumberland and Tyne & Wear			
	1-85937-072-1	£14.99	Feb
Around Newark	1-85937-105-1	£12.99	Feb
Around Oxford	1-85937-096-9	£12.99	Feb
Oxfordshire	1-85937-076-4	£14.99	Feb
Around Shrewsbury	1-85937-110-8	£12.99	Feb
South Devon Coast	1-85937-107-8	£14.99	Feb
Around Southport	1-85937-106-x	£12.99	Feb
West Midlands	1-85937-109-4	£14.99	Feb
Cambridgeshire	1-85937-086-1	£14.99	Mar
County Durham	1-85937-123-x	£14.99	Mar
Cumbria	1-85937-101-9	£14.99	Mar
Down the Severn	1-85937-118-3	£14.99	Mar
Down the Thames	1-85937-121-3	£14.99	Mar
Around Exeter	1-85937-126-4	£12.99	Mar
Around Folkestone	1-85937-124-8	£12.99	Mar
Gloucestershire	1-85937-102-7	£14.99	Mar
Around Great Yarmouth			
	1-85937-085-3	£12.99	Mar
Kent Living Memories	1-85937-125-6	£14.99	Mar
Around Leicester	1-85937-073-x	£12.99	Mar
Around Liverpool	1-85937-051-9	£12.99	Mar
Around Plymouth	1-85937-119-1	£12.99	Mar
Around Portsmouth	1-85937-122-1	£12.99	Mar
Around Southampton	1-85937-088-8	£12.99	Mar
Around Stratford upon Avon			
	1-85937-098-5	£12.99	Mar
Welsh Castles	1-85937-120-5	£14.99	Mar
Canals and Waterways	1-85937-129-9	£17.99	Apr
East Sussex	1-85937-130-2	£14.99	Apr
Exmoor	1-85937-132-9	£14.99	Apr
Farms and Farming	1-85937-134-5	£17.99	Apr
Around Horsham	1-85937-127-2	£12.99	Apr
Ipswich (pb)	1-85937-133-7	£12.99	Apr
Ireland (pb)	1-85937-181-7	£9.99	Apr
London (pb)	1-85937-183-3	£9.99	Apr
New Forest	1-85937-128-0	£14.99	Apr
Scotland	1-85937-182-5	£9.99	Apr
Stone Circles & Ancient Monuments			
	1-85937-143-4	£17.99	Apr
Sussex (pb)	1-85937-184-1	£9.99	Apr
Colchester (pb)	1-85937-188-4	£8.99	May
County Maps of Britain			
	1-85937-156-6 (192pp)	£19.99	May
Around Harrow	1-85937-141-8	£12.99	May
Leicestershire (pb)	1-85937-185-x	£9.99	May
Lincolnshire	1-85937-135-3	£14.99	May
Around Newquay	1-85937-140-x	£12.99	May
Nottinghamshire (pb)	1-85937-187-6	£9.99	May
Redhill to Reigate	1-85937-137-x	£12.99	May
Scilly Isles	1-85937-136-1	£14.99	May
Victorian & Edwardian Yorkshire			
	1-85937-154-x	£14.99	May
Around Winchester	1-85937-139-6	£12.99	May
Yorkshire (pb)	1-85937-186-8	£9.99	May
Berkshire (pb)	1-85937-191-4	£9.99	Jun
Brighton (pb)	1-85937-192-2	£8.99	Jun
Dartmoor	1-85937-145-0	£14.99	Jun
East London	1-85937-080-2	£14.99	Jun
Glasgow (pb)	1-85937-190-6	£8.99	Jun
Kent (pb)	1-85937-189-2	£9.99	Jun
Victorian & Edwardian Kent			
	1-85937-149-3	£14.99	Jun
North Devon Coast	1-85937-146-9	£14.99	Jun
Peak District	1-85937-100-0	£14.99	Jun
Around Truro	1-85937-147-7	£12.99	Jun
Victorian & Edwardian Maritime Album			
	1-85937-144-2	£14.99	Jun
West Sussex	1-85937-148-5	£14.99	Jun

FRITH PRODUCTS & SERVICES

Francis Frith would doubtless be pleased to know that the pioneering publishing venture he started in 1860 still continues today. More than a hundred and thirty years later, The Francis Frith Collection continues in the same innovative tradition and is now one of the foremost publishers of vintage photographs in the world. Some of the current activities include:

Interior Decoration

Today Frith's photographs can be seen framed and as giant wall murals in thousands of pubs, restaurants, hotels, banks, retail stores and other public buildings throughout the country. In every case they enhance the unique local atmosphere of the places they depict and provide reminders of gentler days in an increasingly busy and frenetic world.

Product Promotions

Frith products have been used by many major companies to promote the sales of their own products or to reinforce their own history and heritage. Brands include Hovis bread, Courage beers, Scots Porage Oats, Colman's mustard, Cadbury's foods, Mellow Birds coffee, Dunhill pipe tobacco, Guinness, and Bulmer's Cider.

Genealogy and Family History

As the interest in family history and roots grows world-wide, more and more people are turning to Frith's photographs of Great Britain for images of the towns, villages and streets where their ancestors lived; and, of course, photographs of the churches and chapels where their ancestors were christened, married and buried are an essential part of every genealogy tree and family album.

A series of easy-to-use CD Roms is planned for publication, and an increasing number of Frith photographs will be able to be viewed on specialist genealogy sites. A growing range of Frith books will be available on CD.

The Internet

Already thousands of Frith photographs can be viewed and purchased on the internet. By the end of the year 2000 some 60,000 Frith photographs will be available on the internet. The number of sites is constantly expanding, each focussing on different products and services from the Collection.
Some of the sites are listed below.

www.townpages.co.uk
www.icollector.com
www.barclaysquare.co.uk
www.cornwall-online.co.uk

For background information on the Collection look at the three following sites:

www.francisfrith.com
www.francisfrith.co.uk
www.frithbook.co.uk

Frith Products

All Frith photographs are available Framed or just as Mounted Prints, and can be ordered from the address below. From time to time other products - Address Books, Calendars, Table Mats, Postcards etc - are available.

The Frith Collectors' Guild

In response to the many customers who enjoy collecting Frith photographs we have created the Frith Collectors' Guild. Members are entitled to a range of benefits, including a regular magazine, special discounts and special limited edition products.

For further information: if you would like further information on any of the above aspects of the Frith business please contact us at the address below:
The Francis Frith Collection, Frith's Barn, Teffont, Salisbury, Wiltshire England SP3 5QP.
Tel: +44 (0) 1722 716 376 Fax: +44 (0) 1722 716 881 Email: uksales@francisfrith.com

To receive your FREE Mounted Print

Cut out this Voucher and return it with your remittance for £1.50 to cover postage and handling. Choose any photograph included in this book. Your SEPIA print will be A4 in size, and mounted in a cream mount with burgundy rule lines, overall size 14 x 11 inches.

Order additional Mounted Prints at HALF PRICE (only £7.49 each*)

If there are further pictures you would like to order, possibly as gifts for friends and family, acquire them at half price (no additional postage and handling required).

Have your Mounted Prints framed*

For an additional £14.95 per print you can have your chosen Mounted Print framed in an elegant polished wood and gilt moulding, overall size 16 x 13 inches (no additional postage and handling required).

---

* IMPORTANT!
These special prices are only available if ordered using the original voucher on this page (no copies permitted) and at the same time as your free Mounted Print, for delivery to the same address

---

Voucher for FREE and Reduced Price Frith Prints

Picture no.	Page number	Qty	Mounted @ £7.49	Framed + £14.95	Total Cost
		1	**Free of charge***	£	£
			£	£	£
			£	£	£
			£	£	£
			£	£	£
			£	£	£
				* Post & handling	£1.50
Book Title				**Total Order Cost**	£

Please do not photocopy this voucher. Only the original is valid, so please cut it out and return it to us.

I enclose a cheque / postal order for £ . . . . made payable to 'The Francis Frith Collection' OR please debit my Mastercard / Visa / Switch / Amex card

Number . . . .

Expires . . . . Signature . . . .

Name Mr/Mrs/Ms . . . .

Address . . . .

. . . .

. . . .

. . . . Postcode . . . .

Daytime Tel No . . . .   Valid to 31/12/01

Frith Collectors' Guild

From time to time we publish a magazine of news and stories about Frith photographs and further special offers of Frith products. If you would like 12 months FREE membership, please return this form.

Send completed forms to:
The Francis Frith Collection, Frith's Barn, Teffont, Salisbury, Wiltshire SP3 5QP

The Francis Frith Collectors' Guild

Please enrol me as a member for 12 months free of charge.

Name Mr/Mrs/Ms . . . .

Address . . . .

. . . .

. . . .

. . . . Postcode . . . .

Free Print - see overleaf